My First 1000 Words in ENGLISH

Susan Martineau, Sam Hutchinson, Louise Millar and Catherine Bruzzone

Illustrations by Stu McLellan

Contents

b small publishing
www.bsmall.co.uk

pen

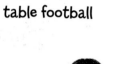
table football

child

reading corner

whiteboard

twins

textbook

teacher

At school

door

clock

bookshelf

tablet

snack

scissors

satchel

computer

 chair

classroom

 ruler

coloured pencils

 alphabet

 glue

 game

 painting

 paintbrush

 paper

 pupil

 rubber

 rucksack

paints

desk

 poster

 head teacher

pencil

kite

pushchair

feather

The park

tree

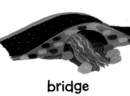
bridge

tadpole

owl

mini-golf

swing

stick

slide

pony

see-saw

sandpit

rowing boat

table tennis

rollerblades

4

 bench

bush

climbing frame

fence

frog

boy

 friends

girl

 goose

 jogger

 park-keeper

 stream

 playground

 pigeon

 skipping rope

 log

 pavilion

 paddling pool

oar

parrot

tiger

At the zoo

zebra

lizard

monkey

shelter

rope

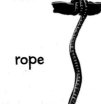
hippopotamus

polar bear

walrus

reindeer

penguin

snake

panda

otter

rhinoceros

meerkat

6

aviary

lion

koala

kangaroo

giraffe

animals

cactus

racoon

elephant

chameleon

burrow

gorilla

crocodile

bat

beaver

wolf

jungle

cage

grizzly bear

The farm

tractor

trailer

field

broom

wellington boots

trough

sheepdog

shepherd

scarecrow

hay

yard

rat

rabbit

sack

quadbike

piglet

pig

beehive

 duck duckling

 mud

 calf

 cow

 chicken

 chick

 barn

 crow

 badger

 farmhouse

 wheat

 orchard

 goat

 kid

 lamb

 sheep

 foal

horse

combine harvester

washing-up

cereal

The kitchen

teapot

beaker

washing machine

plate

saucer

toast

tissues

knife

tea towel

spoon

table

saucepan

tea

sink

stool

water

10

coffee

 bib

cup

 egg cup

 window

 bowl

 breakfast

 apron

 cooker

 fork

 fridge

 glass

 highchair

 pasta

orange juice

 milk

letter

 jam

 wok

11

treehouse

wheelbarrow

In the garden

flower

leaf

worm

watering-can

water butt

snail

wood

axe

rake

spider

wall

shed

saw

trowel

pond

path

12

apple tree

 hedge

 lawn

 gate

 basket

 branch

 garage

 compost heap

 grass

 greenhouse

 hammer

 bird feeder

 hose

 lawnmower

 nail

 toolbox

 plant pot

 vegetable garden

 kitten

 ladder

13

Bathroom and bedroom

shower

towel

washbasin

toothpaste

toothbrush

toilet

toilet paper

alarm clock

bath

sponge

soap

shampoo

sheet

pillow

mobile phone

teddy bear

 bed

 bedside table

 chest of drawers

 blanket

 wardrobe

 cot

 curtains

 desk lamp

 duvet

 hairbrush

 hamster

 mirror

 mat

 jewellery box

 headphones

 house

 comb

 trunk

At home

apartment

furniture

telephone

vacuum cleaner

television

mouse hole

stains

speakers

sofa

sitting room

radio

rug

dog

jug of water

footstool

picture

bottle

napkin

ceiling

coaster

cupboard

cushion

dining room

puppy

dresser

DVD

plant

armchair

vase

floor

key

remote control

cat

mouse

meal

laptop

lampshade

lamp

Beach and under the sea

lighthouse

spade

seagull

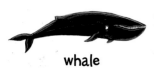
whale

wave

swimming costume

life jacket

sunglasses

suncream

sandcastle

shell

shark

starfish

seaweed

surfboard

surfer

 crab

 bucket

 buoy

 fishing boat

 chips

 deckchair

 beach umbrella

 cliff

 diver

 coral

 dolphin

 fish

candyfloss

jellyfish

sand octopus wreck lobster ball yacht rubber ring dinghy

19

In the countryside

campsite

picnic

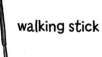
walking stick

walking boots

track

vineyard

tent

river

waterfall

squirrel

signpost

sandwich

beetle

binoculars

rock

paddle

mountain bike

bird

brown bear

butterfly

stones

crane

canoe

caterpillar

swan

cygnet

deer

fire

fishing

fly

forest

fox

mountain

mosquito

map

lake

holiday

hill

Bookshop and toyshop

blocks

dice

xylophone

trumpet

tricycle

toys

till

superhero costume

robot

storybook

model aeroplane

jigsaw

shelf

rocking horse

22

book

cuddly toys

cymbals

castle

drum

dictionary

doll's house

doll

dominoes

stilts

globe

guitar

puppets

purse

recorder

toy train

magic set

money

shop

Transport

vehicles

airport

van

tunnel

boat

ticket

ferry

port

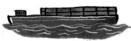
container ship

suitcase

signal

ship

seat

train

rails

rail station

level crossing

aeroplane

digger

dumper truck

brick

bulldozer

helicopter

cement mixer

scaffolding

escalator

bus

fire engine

lift

building site

platform

motorbike

police car

luggage

lorry

In town

roundabout

cinema

postman

postbag

postbox

post office

traffic light

bakery

pedestrian crossing

petshop

road

toilets

umbrella

stall

restaurant

car

factory

bicycle

bin

pavement

flag

butcher's

café

chemist

bank

hotel

library

petrol station

bus stop

office

museum

road sign

market

Party

witch

tiara

sausages

balloon

violin

streamer

queen

princess

prince

mermaid

pirate

party hat

party dress

party blower

giant

music

 cupcakes

 beads

 ice-cream

 pizza

 present

 chocolate

 fairy

 cola

 crown

candle

 knight

 cloak

 ballet shoes

 genie

 king

 fruit juice

magic wand

 lemonade

 lollipop

 magic lamp

 dragon

The supermarket

vegetables

apple

yogurt

trolley

tomato

strawberry

shopping bag

salad

rice

potato

pineapple

pear

peach

orange

onion

mango

lemon

lettuce

aubergine

 banana

 biscuits

 bread

 butter

cabbage

 cake

 carrot

 celery

 cheese

 cherry

 chicken

 corn

 courgette

cucumber

 kiwi

 ham

 grapes

 fruit

 food

fish

 eggs

At the sports centre

sport

race

yoga

whistle

wheelchair

tennis court

tennis

team

starting block

sports kit

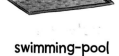
sports bag

swimming-pool

swimming

skis

skiing

shuttlecock

 aerobics

 badminton athletics

 basketball

 changing-room

 football match

 diving board

 football

 racket

 coach

 ball

 goggles

 gymnastics

 scoreboard

 sauna

 referee

goalkeeper

high jump

 long jump

Doing words

standing

walking

watching TV

talking

cooking

sitting

cleaning
your teeth

carrying

pushing

pulling

pointing

playing

painting

jumping

34

reading

 singing

 drawing

 writing

 crawling

 cycling

 dancing

 doing a cartwheel

 doing a handstand

 doing somersaults

 climbing

 drinking

 eating

 getting up

 kissing

 hugging

 having a wash

 running

 going to sleep

35

Your body

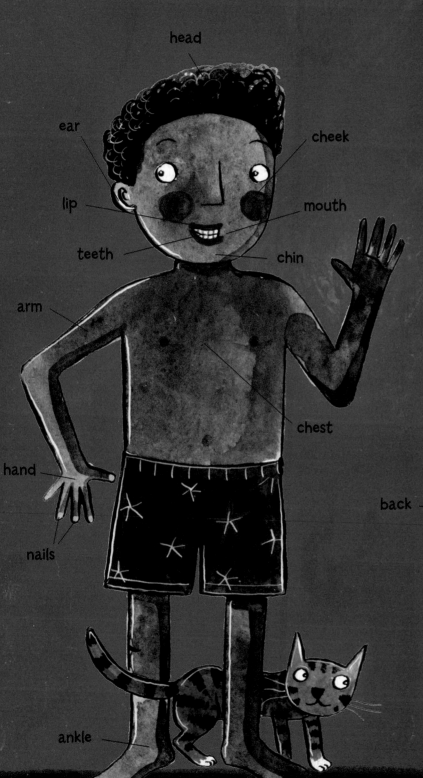

head

ear

cheek

lip

mouth

teeth

chin

arm

chest

hand

nails

ankle

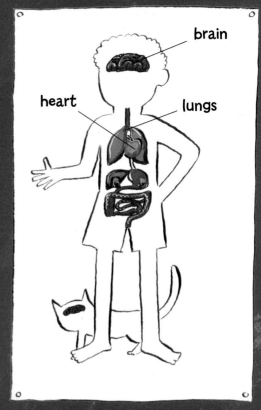

brain

heart

lungs

back

Colours and shapes

easel

palette

sculpture

triangle

frame

cube

circle

crescent

square

rainbow

rectangle

sphere

cylinder

pyramid

hexagon

oval

38

white

black

blue

yellow

brown

violet

artist

turquoise

purple

pink

red

gold

silver

green

art gallery

transparent

pale

orange

multicoloured

grey

Family tree

great-uncle

grandparents

grandpa
grandfather

grandma
grandmother

aunt

uncle

cousins

niece

nephew

great-grandparents

great-aunt

twins

parents

mum
mother

dad
father

My family

brother
son

sister
daughter

baby

triplets

At the hospital

hospital

ambulance

surgeon

visitors

tummy ache

tube

operating theatre

stethoscope

tablets

stitches

waiting-room

headache

42

accident

 bandage

 pager

 chart

 instruments

 corridor

 doctor

 thermometer

 x-ray machine

 injection

crutches

medicine

 nurse

 snack bar

 sling

plaster

 operation

 toothache

 x-ray

Jobs

magician

scientist

zookeeper

sales assistant

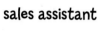
dancer

ticket collector

taxi-driver

secretary

vet

refuse collector

chef

popstar

police officer

plumber

 baker

 builder

 bus driver

 train driver

 dentist

 electrician

 butcher

 farmer

 firefighter

 flight attendant

 footballer

 gardener

 lawyer

 hairdresser

 pilot

 lorry driver

 lifeguard

 lawyer

45

Numbers

How many . . . can you find?

20
twenty

19
nineteen

18
eighteen

17
seventeen

16
sixteen

15
fifteen

14
fourteen

13
thirteen

1
one

2
two

3
three

4
four

5
five

6
six

7
seven

8
eight

9
nine

12

twelve

11

eleven

10

ten

47

Opposites

slow

fast

angry   calm

messy

tidy

wet

dry

noisy

quiet

sad   happy

long   short

ill   healthy

bad good

beautiful ugly

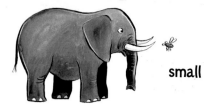
big

small

dirty

clean

first

last

old

young

light

different

same

cold

hot

empty

full

heavy

astronaut

winter

wind

Space, weather and seasons

alien

storm

tornado

sun

star

summer

ocean

space shuttle

snowman

snow

sky

asteroid

UFO

continent

cloud

comet

autumn

Earth

fog

galaxy

hail

ice

lightning

moon

satellite

rocket

rain

orbit

planets

spring

51

Our clothes

handbag

watch

bracelet

shirt

trousers

tights

T-shirt

pyjamas

slippers

shorts

belt

scarf

socks

waistcoat

sandals

ring

shoes

poncho

 boots

 skirt

 cap

 cardigan

bag

 dress

 football boots

 glasses

 gloves

 coat

 jacket

 hat

jumper

make-up

 pocket

 pants

 nightdress

necklace

nail varnish

Additional words

Here are some words that you will find useful as you practise your English at home.
They did not make it into the illustrated scenes in the book so they are gathered here for reference.
These words also appear in the word lists at the back of the book.

left	right	in front of	Mrs.	Mr.	name
me	you	she	her	he	him
January	February	March	April	May	June
July	August	September	October	November	December
Monday	Tuesday	Wednesday	Thursday	Friday	Saturday
Sunday	today	yesterday	morning	afternoon	night
days	months	year	birthday	hundred	thousand
bright	vivid	dark	competition	travel	height
on	behind	under	hug	kiss	weight

Word list

accident
aerobics
aeroplane
afternoon
airport
alarm clock
alien
alphabet
ambulance
angry
animals
ankle
apartment
apple
apple tree
April
apron
arm
armchair
art gallery
artist
asteroid
astronaut
athletics
aubergine
August
aunt
autumn
aviary
axe
baby
back
bad

badger
badminton
bag
baker
bakery
ball
ballet shoes
balloon
banana
bandage
bank
barn
basket
basketball
bat
bath
bathroom
beach
beach umbrella
beads
beaker
beautiful
beaver
bed
bedroom
bedside table
beehive
beetle
behind
belt
bench
bib
bicycle

big
bin
binoculars
bird
bird feeder
biscuits
black
blanket
blocks
blue
boat
body
bone
book
bookshelf
bookshop
boots
bottle
bowl
boy
bracelet
brain
branch
bread
breakfast
brick
bridge
bright
broom
brother
brown
brown bear
bucket

builder
building site
bulldozer
buoy
burrow
bus
bus driver
bus stop
bush
butcher
butcher's
butter
butterfly
cabbage
cactus
café
cage
cake
calf
calm
campsite
candle
candyfloss
canoe
cap
car
cardigan
carrot
carrying
castle
cat
caterpillar
ceiling
celery
cement mixer
cereal
chair

chameleon
changing-room
chart
cheek
cheese
chef
chemist
cherry
chest
chest of drawers
chick
chicken
child
chin
chips
chocolate
cinema
circle
classroom
clean
cleaning your teeth
cliff
climbing
climbing frame
cloak
clock
clothes
cloud
coach
coaster
coat
coffee
cola
cold
colours
comb
combine harvester

comet
competition
compost heap
computer
container ship
continent
cooker
cooking
coral
corn
corridor
cot
coloured pencils
countryside
courgette
cousins
cow
crab
crane
crawling
crescent
crocodile
crow
crown
crutches
cube
cucumber
cuddly toys
cup
cupboard
cupcakes
curtains
cushion
cycling
cygnet
cylinder
cymbals

dad	dry	finger
dancer	duck	fire
dancing	duckling	fire engine
dark	dumper truck	firefighter
daughter	duvet	first
days	DVD	fish
December	ear	fishing
deckchair	Earth	fishing boat
deer	easel	five
dentist	eating	flag
desk	eggs	flight attendant
desk lamp	egg cup	floor
dice	eight	flower
dictionary	eighteen	fly
different	elbow	foal
digger	electrician	fog
dinghy	elephant	food
dining room	eleven	foot
dirty	empty	football
diver	escalator	football boots
diving board	eyes	football match
doctor	face	footballer
dog	factory	footstool
doing a cartwheel	fairy	forest
doing a handstand	family	fork
doing somersaults	family tree	four
doll	farm	fourteen
doll's house	farmer	fox
dolphin	farmhouse	frame
dominoes	fast	Friday
door	father	fridge
dragon	feather	friend
drawing	February	friends
dress	fence	frog
dresser	ferry	fruit
drinking	field	fruit juice
drum	fifteen	full

furniture
galaxy
game
garage
garden
gardener
gate
genie
getting up
giant
giraffe
girl
glass
glasses
globe
gloves
glue
goalkeeper
goat
goggles
going to sleep
gold
good
goose
gorilla
grandfather
grandma
grandmother
grandpa
grandparents
grapes
grass
great-aunt
great-grandparents
great-uncle
green
greenhouse

grey
grizzly bear
guitar
gymnastics
hail
hair
hairbrush
hairdresser
ham
hammer
hamster
hand
handbag
happy
hat
having a wash
hay
he
head
head teacher
headache
headphones
healthy
heart
heavy
hedge
height
helicopter
her
hexagon
high jump
highchair
hill
him
hippopotamus
holiday
home

horse
hose
hospital
hot
hotel
house
hug
hugging
hundred
ice
ice-cream
ill
in front of
injection
instruments
jacket
jam
January
jellyfish
jewellery box
jigsaw
jobs
jogger
jug of water
July
jumper
jumping
June
jungle
kangaroo
key
kid (baby goat)
king
kiss
kissing
kitchen
kite

kitten
kiwi
knee
knife
knight
koala
ladder
lake
lamb
lamp
lampshade
laptop
last
lawn
lawnmower
lawyer
leaf
left
leg
lemonade
lemon
letter
lettuce
level crossing
library
life jacket
lifeguard
lift
light
lighthouse
lightning
lion
lip
lizard
lobster
log
lollipop

long
long jump
lorry
lorry driver
luggage
lungs
magic lamp
magic set
magic wand
magician
make-up
mango
map
March
market
mat
May
me
meal
medicine
meerkat
mermaid
messy
milk
mini-golf
mirror
mobile phone
model aeroplane
Monday
money
monkey
months
moon
morning
mosquito
mother
motorbike

mountain
mountain bike
mouse
mouse hole
mouth
Mr.
Mrs.
mud
multicoloured
mum
museum
music
nail
nail varnish
nails
name
napkin
neck
necklace
nephew
niece
night
nightdress
nine
nineteen
noisy
nose
November
numbers
nurse
oar
ocean
October
octopus
office
old
on

one	peach	port
onion	pear	post office
operating theatre	pedestrian crossing	postbag
operation	pen	postbox
opposites	pencil	poster
orange (colour)	penguin	postman
orange (fruit)	petrol station	potato
orange juice	petshop	present
orbit	picnic	prince
orchard	picture	princess
otter	pig	pulling
oval	pigeon	pupil
owl	piglet	puppets
paddle	pillow	puppy
paddling pool	pilot	purple
pager	pineapple	purse
paintbrush	pink	pushchair
painting	pirate	pushing
painting	pizza	pyjamas
paints	planets	pyramid
pale	plant	quadbike
palette	plant pot	queen
panda	plaster	quiet
pants	plate	rabbit
paper	platform	race
parents	playground	racket
park	playing	racoon
park-keeper	plumber	radio
parrot	pocket	rail station
party	pointing	rails
party blower	polar bear	rain
party dress	police car	rainbow
party hat	police officer	rake
pasta	poncho	rat
path	pond	reading
pavement	pony	reading corner
pavilion	popstar	recorder

rectangle	sandwich	shepherd
red	satchel	ship
referee	satellite	shirt
refuse collector	Saturday	shoes
reindeer	saucepan	shop
remote control	saucer	shopping bag
restaurant	sauna	short
rhinoceros	sausages	shorts
rice	saw	shoulders
right	scaffolding	shower
ring	scarecrow	shuttlecock
river	scarf	signal
road	school	signpost
road sign	scientist	silver
robot	scissors	singing
rock	scoreboard	sink
rocket	sculpture	sister
rocking horse	seagull	sitting
rollerblades	seasons	sitting room
rope	seat	six
roundabout	seaweed	sixteen
rowing boat	secretary	skeleton
rubber ring	see-saw	skiing
rubber	September	skipping rope
rucksack	seven	skirt
rug	seventeen	skis
ruler	shampoo	skull
running	shapes	sky
sack	shark	slide
sad	she	sling
salad	shed	slippers
sales assistant	sheep	slow
same	sheepdog	small
sand	sheet	snack
sandals	shelf	snack bar
sandcastle	shell	snail
sandpit	shelter	snake

snow
snowman
soap
socks
sofa
son
space
space shuttle
spade
speakers
sphere
spider
sponge
spoon
sport
sports bag
sports centre
sports kit
spring
square
squirrel
stains
stall
standing
star
starfish
starting block
stethoscope
stick
stilts
stitches
stones
stool
storm
storybook
strawberry
stream

streamer
suitcase
summer
sun
suncream
Sunday
sunglasses
superhero costume
supermarket
surfboard
surfer
surgeon
swan
swimming
swimming costume
swimming-pool
swing
table
table football
table tennis
tablet
tablets
tadpole
talking
taxi-driver
tea
tea towel
teacher
team
teapot
teddy bear
teeth
telephone
television
ten
tennis
tennis court

tent
textbook
thermometer
thirteen
thousand
three
Thursday
tiara
ticket
ticket collector
tidy
tiger
tights
till
tissues
toast
today
toe
toilet
toilet paper
toilets
tomato
tongue
toolbox
toothache
toothbrush
toothpaste
tornado
towel
town
toy train
toys
toyshop
track
tractor
traffic light
trailer

train

train driver

transparent

transport

travel

tree

treehouse

triangle

tricycle

triplets

trolley

trough

trousers

trowel

trumpet

trunk

T-shirt

tube

Tuesday

tummy

tummy ache

tunnel

turquoise

twelve

twenty

twins

two

UFO

ugly

umbrella

uncle

under

under the sea

uniform

vacuum cleaner

van

vase

vegetable garden

vegetables

vehicles

vet

vineyard

violet

violin

visitors

vivid

waistcoat

waiting-room

walking

walking boots

walking stick

wall

walrus

wardrobe

washbasin

washing machine

washing-up

watch

watching TV

water

water butt

waterfall

watering-can

wave

weather

Wednesday

weight

wellington boots

wet

whale

wheat

wheelbarrow

wheelchair

whistle

white

whiteboard

wind

window

winter

witch

wok

wolf

wood

worm

wreck

writing

x-ray

x-ray machine

xylophone

yacht

yard

year

yellow

yesterday

yoga

yogurt

you

young

zebra

zoo

zookeeper

Published by b small publishing ltd.
Text and illustrations © b small publishing ltd. 2014

2 3 4 5 6 7 8 9 10

British Library Cataloguing-in-Publication Data
A catalogue record for this book is available
from the British Library.

Illustrations: Stu McLellan
Design: Louise Millar
Editorial: Sam Hutchinson and Susan Martineau
Production: Madeleine Ehm
Printed in China by WKT Co. Ltd.

ISBN 978-1-909767-58-4

Please visit our website if you
would like to contact us:
www.bsmall.co.uk